THE BIBLE, CHRISTIANITY, & HOMOSEXUALITY

JUSTIN R. CANNON

The Bible, Christianity, & Homosexuality

Copyright © 2012 Justin R. Cannon

Printed in the United States of America.

ISBN: 1438249616
ISBN-13: 978-1438249612

"If you continue in my word, you are truly my disciples, and you will know the truth, and the truth will make you free."

-Jesus of Nazareth (John 8:31-32)

CONTENTS

1

INTRODUCTION

What does the Bible really say about homosexuality? Should the Church allow the blessing of homosexual marriages/unions? Should a homosexual in a committed, faithful relationship be ordained a priest or even consecrated bishop? What does a traditional understanding of marriage have to do with any of this? What should I tell my friends or relatives who are gay? We all have pondered at least one of these questions at some time or another.

This study is the product of years of research, dialogue, and prayerful reflection. It began when I decided that I needed to know once and for all what the Bible says about homosexuality. There are so many opinions floating around these days about what the Bible does and does not say about homosexuality. Some say, "The Bible clearly condemns homosexuality." Others assert, "Jesus abolished the law and said nothing about homosexuality– if it was so bad wouldn't he have said something?"

There are many fine books on the subject, but not everyone has the time or motivation to read a one hundred plus page book on this topic. Further, there are many cursory pamphlets on this topic, which really do not do the scriptures justice. My hope in writing this was to be comprehensive, yet also concise. Through this study, I offer you a close analysis of the Bible verses that have often been cited in contemporary times with reference to homosexuality. I will also explore homosexuality within the context of Christian tradition.

Regardless of whether or not you are a Bible scholar; whether or not you can read Greek; or if you know everything or nothing about Christian tradition, you will be able to follow this study of *The Bible, Christianity, & Homosexuality*.

2

TERMINOLOGY

Homosexual

The English word *homosexual* is a compound word made from the Greek word *homo*, meaning "the same," and the Latin term *sexualis*, meaning "sex." The term *homosexual* is of modern origin, and it was not until about a hundred and fifty years ago that it was first used. There is no word in biblical Greek or Hebrew that is equivalent to the English word homosexual. The 1946 Revised Standard Version (RSV) New Testament was the first translation to use the word homosexual.

Sodomite

There is no word in biblical Greek or Hebrew for "sodomy" or "sodomite" as these terms have been used in contemporary times. A Sodomite would have been simply an inhabitant of Sodom, just as a Moabite would have been an inhabitant of Moab. Any translation of New Testament passages that make use of the words *sodomy* or *sodomites*, other than to simply refer to inhabitants of the town, are clear interpretations and not faithful translations.

Arsenokoites (ἀρσενοκοίτης)

This Greek noun is formed from the joining together of the Greek adjectival prefix for male (*arseno-*) and the Greek word for beds (*koites*). Literally then it would mean, "male beds." It is found in 1 Timothy 1:10 and 1 Corinthians 6:9. This is the first appearance of the word in preserved Greek literature, and outside of these two verses this word does not appear at all in the Bible. The meaning of the word *arsenokoites* in both 1 Corinthians 6:9 and 1 Timothy 1:10 is debated. Because of the obscurity of this word and the lack of outside sources to shed light on its meaning, we must derive its meaning from the Pauline texts.

3

PASSAGE I: THE SODOM ACCOUNT

The story of Sodom is an appropriate text to begin with, as it has taken a central role in the study of homosexuality. We must first understand the context of this account. God, according to this account, sent two angels to warn Abraham's nephew, Lot, about the approaching destruction of Sodom. If we stop here for a moment we will see that even before sending the angels, God had intended to destroy Sodom. Whatever the reason was for the city's destruction, it had to do with the sin of Sodom before this event.

So, the angels came to the city of Sodom and Lot welcomed them to his home and prepared a meal for them. Then a grouping townsfolk, including the men, surrounded the house and asked where the angels who had come to the house were. They basically shouted, "Where are those men who came to your house? We want to have sex with them!" Lot refused but offered his daughters instead, giving the reason: "Look, I have two daughters who have never slept with a man. Let me bring them out to you, and you can do what you like with them. Don't do anything to these men, for they have come under the protection of my roof" (19:8). The crowd of men insisted on what they wanted and tried to break through the door. The angels ended up pulling Lot into the house and blinding the crowd.

First of all, in interpreting this event we must take into account the entire situation. Whatever is happening here it is a form of rape. The crowd of men wished to sexually assault or "gangbang" the angels. The situation is also sewn through with appalling violence. Many assert that Lot's offer of his daughters instead of the male angels implies that homosexual sex would have been worse than heterosexual sex, but Lot himself gives his reason for his action: "Don't do anything to these men, *for they have come under the protection of my roof.*" In our time, this does not make sense at all, but in Lot's day, hospitality was a nearly sacred contract, and it is that distinction that Lot expresses: *the visitors are his guests.*

11

In addition to the plain context of this story, namely that of rape, there are a few additional elements that shed some light on the fact that this story has nothing whatsoever to do with homosexuality.

For one, it is often asserted, that Genesis 19:4 depicts solely the men of the town sexually pursuing the angels. An example of this would be the New International Version (NIV) of the Bible that reads, "Before they had gone to bed, all the men from every part of the city of Sodom—both young and old—surrounded the house." If you look at the original Hebrew text, and even early Greek translations, the word translated into English as "men" can be inclusive of the women as well, much like the historical, antiquated use of the term "man" or "mankind" or the Spanish third person plural *ellos* and French *ils*. This is somewhat rendered in the King James Version (KJV), which translates this verse, "But before they lay down, *the men of the city, even the men of Sodom*, compassed the house round, both old and young, all the people from every quarter" (italics mine). In other words, it wasn't just the men of the city, but all the inhabitants, men and women, young and old alike.

Even in light of this, if somewhere were to claim that the distinction is gender-based, he or she could only assert that homosexual rape of angels is worse than heterosexual rape. To use this story to condemn loving, committed, monogamous homosexual relationships is unfounded and truly stretching this story outside of its historical framework, but that is exactly what has happened. As Jeffrey S. Silker, in reference to such distortion of this text, wrote in his article in *Theology Today*, "As for the Sodom and Gomorrah story, one can certainly conclude that homosexual rape (just like heterosexual rape)…is an abomination before God, but it does not follow from this that all expressions of homosexuality are prohibited (David's sin of adultery with Bathsheba does not make all heterosexual expressions sinful!)."[1]

If we are left wondering, then, what the sin of Sodom really was– so horrendous that God had decided to destroy the town– we only need to look to Ezekiel 16:49-50. The NIV Bible, one of the more evangelical translations of the Bible, renders these verses: "Now this

was the *sin of your sister Sodom*: She and her daughters were arrogant, overfed and unconcerned; they did not help the poor and needy. They were haughty and did detestable things before me. Therefore I did away with them as you have seen." Other translations are equally revealing, and just as explicitly lay out the *sin of Sodom* as inhospitality, greed, and arrogance. Those are the sins of Sodom.

If that is not convincing enough, let us look to the words of none other than Jesus himself in the Gospel of Luke. When he sent out his disciples, he compared the fate of the *inhospitable* towns that would not receive them to the fate Sodom, saying that it will be worse off for these towns that do not welcome the disciples. He explains:

> "Whenever you enter a town and its people welcome you, eat what is set before you; cure the sick who are there, and say to them, 'The kingdom of God has come near to you' But whenever you enter a town and they do not welcome you, go out into its streets and say, 'Even the dust of your town that clings to our feet, we wipe off in protest against you. Yet know this: the kingdom of God has come near.' I tell you, on that day it will be more tolerable for Sodom than for that town" (Luke 10:8-12).

The sin of Sodom was that of greed, inhospitality, rape, and arrogance. In no way can this account be read with reference to homosexuality, much less loving, committed, homosexual relationships.

AN INTERESTING FACT

In the 1508 Wycliffe translation of the Bible into Middle English, the Greek word *arsenokoites* (ἀρσενοκοίτης), often translated as homosexuals, was translated "synn of Sodom." Wycliffe's own interpretation was that *arsenokoites* had something to do with the Sodom story, though nothing is implied as such in the New Testament text. The author could very well have written "sin of Sodom" if he had wanted to.

If your Bible translation has the translation "sodomites," it is an

interpretation and not a faithful translation. We will look more closely at the word *arsenokoites* below in our study of the 1 Corinthians and 1 Timothy texts; however, it is remarkable to see how the story of Sodom, filled with rape and violence, has taken such a central role surrounding the topic of homosexuality and more precisely in the development of the word "sodomite" to what it means today.

4

PASSAGE II: 1 TIMOTHY 1:8-10

"Now we know that the law is good, if any one uses it lawfully, understanding this, that the law is not laid down for the just but for the lawless and disobedient, for the ungodly and sinners, for the unholy and profane, for murderers of fathers and murderers of mothers, for manslayers, immoral persons, sodomites, kidnappers, liars, perjurers, and whatever else is contrary to sound doctrine..."

The word translated as *sodomites* in the list above is none other than the Greek word *arsenokoites*. Right now we should ask, "What exactly does this word mean?" Just as you or I might do when going shopping, it is not uncommon when writing lists to group common things together. If you look closely at 1 Timothy 1:9-10, you can see that there are structural pairs that are reflected below in the English as well as in the Greek– the original language of the New Testament:

1 Timothy 1:9-10 (RSV) – English

Row A	lawless	and	disobedient
Row B	ungodly	and	sinners
Row C	unholy	and	profane
Row D	murderers of fathers	murderers of mothers	manslayers
Row E	immoral persons	sodomites	kidnappers
Row F	liars	perjurers	

1 Timothy 1:9-10 (RSV) – Greek

The Greek is provided for reference purposes only.
If you do not read Greek, just pay attention to the English chart.

Row A	ἀνόμοις	καὶ	ἀνυποτάκτοις
Row B	ἀσεβέσι	καὶ	ἁμαρτωλοῖς
Row C	ἀνοσίοις	καὶ	βεβήλοις
Row D	πατρολῴαις	μητρολῴαις	ἀνδροφόνοις
Row E	πόρνος	ἀρσενοκοίτης	ἀνδραποδιστής
Row F	ψεύστης	ἐπίορκος	

As you will notice in either chart, there is an obvious relationship between the words in each row. The chart below illustrates how the words in each row are either synonyms or closely related in some manner:

Row A	*lawless* & *disobedient*	=	two synonyms
Row B	*ungodly* & *sinners*	=	two synonyms
Row C	*unholy* & *profane*	=	two synonyms
Row D	*murderers of fathers, murderers of mothers, manslayers*	=	three types of murderers
Row E	*Immoral persons, sodomites, kidnappers*	=	? (see below)
Row F	*liars & perjurers*	=	two synonyms

The relationship between the words in rows A–D and row F are evident, but what about Row E? What do "immoral persons, sodomites, and kidnappers" have in common? To answer this question beyond a shadow of a doubt, we will need to explore the Greek. The three Greek words present in line E are: *pornos* (πόρνος), *arsenokoites* (ἀρσενοκοίτης), and *andrapodistes* (ἀνδραποδιστής).

Some commonly read Bible translations include the King James Version (KJV), New International Version (NIV), New King James (NKJ), Revised Standard Version (RSV), and New English Bible (NEB). These words were, respectively, translated in the following manner:

	pornos	*arsenokoites*	*andrapodistes*
KJV	whoremonger	"them that defile themselves with mankind"	men-stealers
NIV	adulterers	perverts	slave traders
NKJV	fornicators	sodomites	kidnappers
RSV	immoral persons	sodomites	kidnappers
NEB	fornicators	perverts	kidnappers

As we see there is no clear-cut agreement as to what these words mean, though the above translations agree on the general sense of such words. See Appendix 1 at the end of this booklet for a more complete list of the countless ways *arsenokoites* has been translated through time. To determine the precise meanings of these words, we will use a *lexicon*. A lexicon is a scholarly dictionary used to determine the general meaning of biblical words. A search through *The KJV New Testament Greek Lexicon* (Thayer and Smith), available online at biblestudytools.com and in the public domain, yields the following information:

Pornos derives from the verb *pernemi* meaning "to sell" and the following three definitions are given:
1. a male who prostitutes his body to another's lust for hire
2. a male prostitute
3. a male who indulges in unlawful sexual intercourse, a fornicator

Andrapodistes, the third word, returns the following definitions:
1. slave-dealer, kidnapper, man-stealer
   a. of one who unjustly reduces free males to slavery
   b. of one who steals the slaves of others and sells them.

The third term, *arsenokoites*, is a term Paul invented from the Greek words for male (*arseno-*) and beds (*koites*). It's meaning is highly debated and cannot be easily defined like the two terms above since it did not occur in Greek writing before Paul coined it. What follows, is a list of different ways this word has been translated through time.

Notice the diversity covering everything from child molesters to "practicing" homosexuals.

Koine Greek	56 A.D.	*arsenokoitai*
Latin Vulgate	405 A.D.	*masculorum concubitores*
Wyclif	1508 A.D.	synne of Sodom
Tyndale	1525 A.D.	abusers of themselves with mankynde
Geneva	1560 A.D.	bouggerers
King James	1611 A.D.	abusers of themselves with mankind
Young	1898 A.D.	sodomites
Jerusalem	1966 A.D.	child molesters (German Version)
NIV	1973 A.D.	homosexual offenders
New American	1987 A.D.	practicing homosexuals
New Living	1996 A.D.	homosexuals

To understand this term, *arsenokoites*, better, we need to look at both parts of the word. *Arseno-* is an adjectivial prefix meaning "male." In Greek, the word *koitai*, literally meaning beds, is commonly used as a euphemism for someone who has sex with another. Examples of this include *doulokoites* (one who has sex with slaves), *metrokoites* (one who has sex with their mother), *polukoites* (one who has sex with many people). Literally, we could translate this as "a man who has sex" or "male bedder." The meaning of this word becomes clearer when we reconsider the list of terms. We have, first of all, a male prostitute, the "male-bedder" (*arsenokoitai*), and the slave dealer. The New American Bible offers a footnote for 1 Corinthians 6:9 (where *arsenokoitai* also appears) that might shed some light on the historical context of the time:

"The Greek word translated as boy prostitutes designated catamites, i.e. boys or young men who were kept for purposes of prostitution, a practice not uncommon in the Greco-Roman world. In Greek mythology this was the function of Ganymede, the "cupbearer of the gods," whose Latin name was Catamus. The term translated practicing homosexuals *refers to males*

who indulged in homosexual practices with such boys…" [2]

It was a common practice for men of Paul's time to have slave "pet" boys whom they sexually exploited. Dr. Ralph Blair explains, "The desired boys were prepubescent or at least without beards so that they seemed like females."[3] Today, this practice is referred to as pedophilia. Regardless, we know that the *pornos* is a prostitute, and most probably a young boy prostitute.

Keeping this in mind, let's look back at what we have so far: the young male prostitute, the "male-bedder," and the slave dealer. This contextual dynamic leads one to understand *arsenokoites* as being the one who sleeps with the prostitute—the man who literally lies on the *bed* with him. It is as if Paul were saying, "male prostitutes, males who lie [with them], and slave dealers [who procure them]."[4] Not only does the syntactical and historical context point to this understanding, but also the very literal sense of the word *arsenokoites* itself.

If this translation of *arsenokoites* is correct, it should also make logical sense where it is also used in 1 Corinthians 6:9, either confirming or refuting this understanding of *arsenokoites*.

5

PASSAGE III: 1 CORINTHIANS 6:9-10

"Do you not know that the unrighteous will not inherit the kingdom of God? Do not be deceived; neither the immoral, nor idolaters, nor adulterers, **nor sexual perverts***, nor thieves, nor the greedy, nor drunkards, nor revilers, nor robbers will inherit the kingdom of God."*

The term translated "sexual perverts" above is actually two different words. The first word is *malakoi* and the second term is that mysterious word *arsenokoitai* (ἀρσενοκοῖται). Some commonly read Bible translations are as follow:

	malakoi	*arsenokoitai*
KJV	effeminate	abusers of themselves with mankind
NIV	male prostitutes	homosexual offenders
NKJ	homosexuals	sodomites
RSV (1977)	sexual perverts	
RSV (1989)	male prostitutes	
Jerusalem	catamites	sodomites

Be sure to consult the Appendix 1 at the end of this booklet for a more complete list of the countless ways *malakoi* and *arsenokoites* have been translated through time.

The term malakoi, as an adjective, literally means "soft." In Matthew 11:8 it has been used as an adjective in reference to John the Baptist's clothing. In this text, however, it is used as a noun and its meaning is debated. Does our understanding of *arsenokoitai* as revealed in 1

Timothy 1:10 as men who sleep with boy prostitutes make sense next to this word *malakos* which is translated by both NIV and RSV as male prostitutes? The Jerusalem Bible even translates the term *malakos* as *catamites*, those young soft prepubescent "pet" boys mentioned earlier.

The syntactical and historical context of 1 Timothy 1:10 reveals the meaning of the word *arsenokoitai* as men who sleep with boy prostitutes, and the fact this also fits the context of 1 Corinthians 6:9 seems to confirm that we have found the meaning of these obscure words. It makes perfect sense that Paul would rebuke not only the prostitute, but also the "male-bedder" or the man who sleeps with that prostitute. As we see, these two verses are about this practice of prostitution and probably pedophilia.

6

PASSAGE IV: ROMANS 1:24-27

"Therefore God gave them up in the lusts of their hearts to impurity, to the dishonoring of their bodies among themselves, because they exchanged the truth about God for a lie and worshiped and served the creature rather than the Creator, who is blessed for ever! Amen. For this reason God gave them up to dishonorable passions. Their women exchanged natural relations for unnatural, and the men likewise gave up natural relations with women and were consumed with passion for one another, men committing shameless acts with men and receiving in their own persons the due penalty for their error."

To understand what exactly Paul is writing about, we must look at the event as a whole and not isolate a mere portion of it. Each verse in this story gives us a unique glimpse into the complete context of the account:

- **Verse 24:** "Therefore, God gave them up in the *lusts of their hearts* to impurity." If we are painting a picture of this account, it begins with the image of LUST.

- **Verse 25:** "...they exchanged the truth about God for a *lie* and *worshiped and served the creature* rather than the Creator." Now there is a LIE as well as IDOLATRY involved (i.e. worshipping something other than God).

- **Verse 26:** "God gave them up to *dishonorable passions...*" Now DISHONORABLE PASSIONS are presented.

Looking back at this now we see this as a situation of lust, lies, idolatry, and dishonorable passions. Clearly, this account is about

more than just sexual sin, but sexual sin within a very specific context.

- **Verses 26-27:** "Their women exchanged natural relations for unnatural, and the men likewise gave up natural relations with women and were consumed with passion for one another..."

Looking at the men first will help to clarify the passage: "The men likewise gave up natural relations with women..." It is easy to overlook what this is saying because of the interpretation that has been ingrained into our minds through poor teaching, but read that carefully. They *gave up* natural relations with women, and then had sexual relations with on another. There is a movement from A) having natural relations with women to B) giving up those relations and having sexual relations with men. The word translated as "gave up" is the Greek word *aphentes* (ἀφέντες) meaning: *to give up, leave behind, forsake, or divorce.* The question must be asked: How can you give up something you do not have? How can you divorce yourself something you are not bound to?

The men Paul was writing about, he explains had what was regarded for them as natural relationships with women. Basically, today we would say these were heterosexual men– men who are naturally sexually attracted to women. These men, we see, turned their backs on their wives and were consumed with passion for one another. The women in the account did likewise. Paul is not talking about people who have had an attraction to the same sex since a young age, which is the case for many homosexuals today, but men who turned from relationships with women, who were filled with lust and idolatrous passions, and engaged in homosexual sex.

Why would these men do that? As any biblical scholar will tell you: "Context is everything." This is a situation of lust, falsehood, idolatry, and dishonorable passions. In this account there are a number of men and a number of women. Both an accurate reading of this text, and a little historical knowledge would identify this situation as an orgy, not uncommon in the Greco-Roman world. Just look at the language: everyone is filled with lust and "dishonorable passions" having sex with whomever, however.

But why would Paul be talking about orgies? A little research into pagan religious practices contemporary to Paul uncovers the pagan practice of "sacred sexual orgies." Baal was the Canaanite deity that was worshipped with sexual orgies on Mount Peor in Moab, a pagan practice with which Paul would have been familiar. Apparently, during these "sacred" orgies entire families would have sex with no regard for familial bonds, gender, or age. It makes complete sense for Paul to condemn such practices. With this contextual understanding let us read this story again:

> *"Therefore God gave them up in the lusts of their hearts to impurity, to the dishonoring of their bodies among themselves, because they exchanged the truth about God for a lie and worshiped and served the creature rather than the Creator, who is blessed for ever! Amen. For this reason God gave them up to dishonorable passions. Their women exchanged natural relations for unnatural, and the men likewise gave up natural relations with women and were consumed with passion for one another, men committing shameless acts with men and receiving in their own persons the due penalty for their error."*

Anyone who isolates verses 26 and 27 to condemn homosexual relations as unnatural is projecting their own prejudice into these verses and reading this letter entirely outside of context. Even if we were to isolate those verses, they could only be used to condemn heterosexuals who go against their own nature and engage in homosexual activity. As Peter J. Gomes, preacher to Harvard University, further clarifies in his book *The Good Book*, "It is not clear that Saint Paul distinguished, as we must, between homosexual persons and heterosexual persons who behave like homosexuals, *but what is clear is that what is 'unnatural' is the one behaving after the manner of the other*"[5] (italics mine). Interestingly enough, one could argue, in light of this understanding that it would be a sin for a homosexual to engage in heterosexual sex.

PASSAGE V: GENESIS 1-2

"God created Adam and Eve, not Adam and Steve!" In so many places I have either read or heard the above refrain used by Christians trying to "prove" that homosexuality is wrong. You cannot really argue with them about God creating Adam and Eve in the Biblical creation account. In *that* sense, then, they are right. But, one must ask what exactly is revealed by this Creation account. In *The Good Book*, The Rev. Peter Gomes writes:

> *"[T]he authors of Genesis were intent upon answering the question 'Where do we come from?' Then, as now, the only plausible answer is from the union of a man and a woman... The creation story in Genesis does not pretend to be a history of anthropology or of every social relationship. It does not mention friendship, for example, and yet we do not assume that friendship is condemned or abnormal. It does not mention the single state, and yet we know that singleness is not condemned, and that in certain religious circumstances it is held in very high esteem."*[6]

In other words, Adam and Eve's relationship is the only one that would make sense for a account on creation. This is a story about where humanity came from, and only a heterosexual, procreative relationship would be appropriate for this particular story. This does not mean a procreative relationship is for everyone, or that God intends such for every, just that that is from whence humanity has come. Keep in mind that many of the saints and even Jesus lived a solitary, celibate life that does not conform to the model of the creation account. As such, we must read this account for what it is and not as God's infallible guide to all human relationships. If someone, in spite of this, were to base his or her opinion of homosexuality on the Creation story alone, their stance would not only be out of context, but also based on a weak argument.

PASSAGE VI: LEVITICUS 18:22

"Thou shalt not lie with a man as with a woman; it is an abomination."
(KJV)

"Do not lie with a man as one lies with a woman; that is detestable."
(NIV)

"Homosexuality is absolutely forbidden, for it is an enormous sin."
(Living Bible)

It must be acknowledged before we delve into a study of this passage that the *Living Bible* is obviously an interpretation and by no means could it be considered a translation. Beware of Bibles which try to pass mere interpretation as supposed "translations" of the scriptures. In any serious study of Leviticus 18:22, one must look closely at the historical context of this law in order to understand what the original author was referencing. The book of Leviticus is a part of the Hebrew Law and contains everything from commandments for men not to shave the edges of their beards (Lev 19:27); orders not to have intercourse during menstruation (Lev 18:19); not to harvest different crops in the same field (Lev 19:19); as well as numerous dietary laws.

In order to understand this particular law we must look first at the Hebrew Law and how it relates to Christians, an issue the early church faced when Gentiles were being converted. Second, we will look at the eighteenth chapter of Leviticus as a whole, and particularly how this law is a part of the Levitical holiness code. Lastly, we will end this section with a careful examination of Leviticus 18:22.

THE LAW

The early church was faced with the question of whether or not the Levitical laws apply to Christians. Many Gentiles were being converted to Christianity, yet they were not circumcised, nor did they follow the Law that God had given to the Israelites. It was through the observation of the Law that Jews considered themselves justified before God. In reading Paul's letters to the Romans, the Galatians, the Corinthians, the Colossians, and the Hebrews we find a consistent claim that "no one is justified before God by the law" (Galatians 3:10). Paul writes the following in reference to the law:

> *"Likewise, my brethren, you have died to the law through the body of Christ, so that you may belong to another, to him who has been raised from the dead in order that we may bear fruit for God. While we were living in the flesh, our sinful passions, aroused by the law, were at work in our members to bear fruit for death. But now we are discharged from the law, dead to that which held us captive, so that we serve not under the old written code but in the new life of the Spirit"* (Romans 7:4-6).

> *"Now before faith came, we were confined under the law, kept under restraint until faith should be revealed. So that the law was our custodian until Christ came, that we might be justified by faith. But now that faith has come, we are no longer under a custodian* [i.e. The Law]. *For in Christ Jesus you are all sons of God, through faith"* (Galatians 3:23-26).

Other New Testament Scriptures on the Law include: 2 Corinthians 3:6; Colossians 2:13-15; Hebrews 8:8-13, Romans 10:1-4. In the second chapter of his letter to the Galatians he confronts Peter who has been forcing Gentiles to follow the Jewish law (Galatians 2:14), and he goes on to boldly assert:

> *"We ourselves, who are Jews by birth and not Gentile sinners, yet who know that a man is not justified by works of the law but through faith in Jesus Christ, even we have believed in Christ Jesus, in order to be justified by faith in Christ, and not by works of the law, because by works of the law shall no one be justified"* (RSV Galatians 2:15-16).

Paul was even persecuted for this deeply held conviction that as Christians, we are no longer held to the Levitical laws, but are justified through faith in Jesus Christ.

If we are "not under the law" does that mean we can lie, cheat, steal, etc.? In Romans 6:15 Paul answers this question, "By no means!" Did not Christ himself in Matthew 5:17 say that he came not to abolish the law, but to fulfill it? So what is the fulfillment of the law? Jesus was once asked, "Rabbi, which is the greatest commandment in the law?" Jesus replied, "You shall love the Lord your God with all your heart, and with all your soul, and with all your mind. This is the great and first commandment. And a second is like it: You shall love your neighbor as yourself. On these two commandments depend all the law and the prophets" (Matthew 22:36-40). The fulfillment of all the law and prophets is the higher law of love, given to us by Christ. Paul would later echo this idea in Romans as he wrote:

> *"Owe no one anything, except to love one another; for he who loves his neighbor has fulfilled the law. The commandments, 'You shall not commit adultery, You shall not kill, You shall not steal, You shall not covet,' and any other commandment, are summed up in this sentence, 'You shall love your neighbor as yourself.' Love does no wrong to a neighbor; therefore love is the fulfilling of the law"* (Romans 13:8-10).

THE HOLINESS CODE

There are over 600 laws in the Old Testament and the book of Leviticus contains many of such laws (For a list of the 613 laws recognized by many contemporary Jews, visit jewfaq.org/613.htm). The book of Leviticus is a part of what is described as "The Holiness Code," which was given to protect the Israelites from idolatry and to distinguish them from pagan cultures.

Leviticus 18 begins, "And the Lord said to Moses, 'Say to the people of Israel, I am the Lord your God. You shall not do as they do in the land of Egypt, where you dwelt, and you shall not do as they do in the land of Canaan, to which I am bringing you. You shall not walk in their statutes. You shall do my ordinances and keep my statutes and walk in them. I am the Lord your God...'" (Leviticus 18:1-4). This introduction of Leviticus 18 clearly maintains that these laws were given to distinguish them from the ways of the people in Egypt and those in Canaan.

The Old Testament, as has been mentioned, was initially a part of the Hebrew Scriptures of the Jewish people. The *Septuagint* was an ancient translation of the Old Testament (circa 200 B.C.) from its original Hebrew into Greek. It was the "version" of the Old Testament that the New Testament writers often quoted when they cited Old Testament scriptures. The Hebrew word in Levticus 18:22 translated into English as "abomination" was translated in the *Septuagint* as the Greek word *bdelugma* (βδέλυγμα). A quick search through a lexicon for the word *bdelugma* brings up the following definition:

1. a foul thing, a detestable thing
     a.   a. of idols and things pertaining to idolatry

This points to the understanding that this specific law has to do with a matter of ritual purity and with the Hebrews not being like the idolatrous Babylonians or Canaanites. It probably refers to either the sacred orgies involved in the worship of the god Baal, sacred temple prostitutes, or some other form of idolatry (see below).

ABUSIVE SEX

"Thou shalt not lie with a man __as with a woman__; it is an abomination." (KJV)

"Do not lie with a man __as one lies with a woman__; that is detestable." (NIV)

Translated literally from Hebrew Leviticus 18:22 reads: *"And with a male you shall not lay lyings of a woman."* The only way of making sense of this is to insert something to produce a smoother, more coherent

32

English translation. For example, one can insert "as the" or "in the" after the first *lay* as showed below:

"And with a male you shall not lay [as the] lyings of a woman."

"And with a male you shall not lay [in the] lyings of a woman."

Some affirm that this law is quite straightforward. Clearly from the previous sixteen verses, we know that these laws were written to men. Thus, some may say, this law forbids men to "lie with", or have sex with, other men. This interpretation is flawed as it entirely ignores the phrase "as with a woman." These four words cannot simply be understood to refer to lying sexually, since that is already indicated in the Hebrew word translated "to lie with." Since the verb translated "to lie with" already denotes sexual activity, if the above interpretation were what the author meant he could have just written, "Thou shalt not lie with a man; it is an abomination."

The phrase "as with a woman" must have been added for some reason, and we must understand the context of this law to understand it fully. The status of women in that time was much lower than that of men, and women were even considered property of their husbands. This belief regarding gender relations is rejected by most of the Christian church today, but in order to make sense of this specific Jewish law we must keep in mind this context in which it was written.

Rabbi Arthur Waskow explains, "The whole structure of sexuality in the Torah assumes a dominant male and a subordinate female."[7] Further, in such patriarchal societies women were considered property of men, and were "obedient" to their husbands. In having sex, therefore, one should not be shocked that men would often have been dominating and controlling in sexual encounters. In other words, woman did what the man wanted and how the man wanted it.

For a man to be treated in that way (i.e. as a woman) within the Jewish culture of the time, the man would have be taking a lower status, as well as being sexually dominated and controlled. To do so would have been reducing him to property and in effect defiling the image of God, which man was considered in that culture. "Thou shalt not lie with a man as with a woman; it is an abomination" (KJV). Contextually understood, the meaning of this verse is clear. It is akin to saying: You shall not sexually use a man like property. You shall no sexually subjugate a man as one does with women.

This does not mean that the author is endorsing other forms of sex between men. We can tell from this study, though, that he is not writing about loving, committed, gay relationships. Rather, as would be expected, the author is writing about abusive sexual practices common in his day and age. Just as when you and I write critiques of our culture, we are writing about practices we see and familiar with. This Hebrew author would have been familiar with the male temple prostitutes, and the activity described is exactly how men would have treated the male temple prostitutes—in a controlling and abusive manner. That is also how individuals would have been treated in the sacred sexual orgies with which Baal was worshiped. They would have had sex with other men "as with a women"– using them in self-centered ways.

A NEW TESTAMENT CONNECTION

Earlier, in our study of Paul's coinage of the term *arsenokoites*, it was clear that Paul always uses this term following a word for a young boy prostitute (i.e. pornos in 1 Corinthians 6:9 and *malakoi* in 1 Timothy 1:10). If we look closely at the Greek Septuagint translation of Leviticus 18:22 (circa 200 B.C.), there is an interesting connection between this Levitical law and that unique term that Paul coined, *arsenokoites*.

The chart below shows a layout of the Greek Septuagint version of this verse, a transliteration of the Greek, and its English equivalent:

καὶ	μετὰ	ἄρσενος	οὐ	κοιμηθήσῃ	κοίτην	γυναικός
kai	meta	arsenos	ou	koimethese	koiten	gynaikos
and	with	male	not	lay	bed	woman

In the chart, notice the close proximity of the words *arsenos* (ἄρσενος) and *koiten* (κοίτην). These two words, found merely two words apart from each other in this Levitical law, are the very words that Paul combined when he coined the term *arsenokoites* (ἀρσενοκοίτης). Our study of the term *arsenokoites* indicates that Paul used it to denote men who consorted with young boy prostitutes. I am convinced that Paul was looking at this law when he coined this term. His usage of the term indicates that he understood Leviticus 18:22 to be speaking of temple prostitution. This is consistent with our study of the cultural and social context of Leviticus 18:22, wherein men would have been using other men in a sexually exploitative manner, not unlike how the male temple prostitutes would have been "used" by the men who hired them. This seems to affirm the understanding of Paul's usage of *arsenokoitai* as a man who sleeps with male prostitutes, and Paul's usage of that terms seems to corroborate this understanding of what it meant in that time to "lie with a man *as with a woman.*" Both passages appear to be condemning forms of sexual abuse. It makes sense, then, that Paul would have used words from the Levitical law for coining a term to refer to the cohorts of male prostitutes.

As we see, this Levitical law is not as simple as it appears. First of all, we know from Paul's writing that we have "died to" and are "discharged from the law" (Romans 7:4-6). We also know that "love is the fulfilling of the law" (Romans 13:10). Second, we understand that Leviticus is a part of the Holiness code, which was written to distinguish the Israelites from the Canaanites and Moabites. Lastly, we see that Leviticus 18:22 has to do with abusive cultic practices, and says nothing pertaining the issue we are faced with today—that of loving and committed homosexual relationships.

SUMMARY OF THE SCRIPTURES

As we see, the Bible really does not fully address the topic of homosexuality. In the city of Sodom, same-gender sexual behavior is mentioned within the context of rape and precisely raping angels, and in Romans 1:24-27 we find it mentioned within the context of idolatry (Baal worship) involving lust and dishonorable passions. Both 1 Corinthians 6:9 and 1 Timothy 1:10 talk about same-gender sexual behavior in the context of prostitution and possibly pedophilia, not uncommon in the Greco-Roman world.

Nowhere, however, does the Bible come close to condemning a loving and committed homosexual relationship. To use the Bible to condemn such a relationship, as we see, involves a projection of ones own bias into the Biblical texts and a stretching of these texts beyond their original intent. Historically, though, the Bible has been taken out of context and twisted to oppress almost every minority one could imagine including women, those with mental disabilities, African Americans, children, slaves, Jews, and the list goes on. Do we truly understand the greatest commandments…

> *"You shall love the Lord your God with all your heart, and with all your soul, and with all your mind. This is the great and first commandment. And a second is like it, You shall love your neighbor as yourself. On these two commandments depend all the law and the prophets."* (Matthew 22:36-40)

9

TRADITION & MARRIAGE

Tradition is very clear, however, and has held that marriage is a sacrament designed for a very specific purpose, right? The following is taken from the article *Homosexual Marriage* by United Methodist clergyman Tex Sample and is reprinted with permission:

"To address Christian homosexual marriage, attention must be turned to the tradition of the church, and here I am indebted to the work of Daniel M. Bell Jr. St. Augustine is the major figure in the teaching of the church on marriage. For him marriage is an office, a duty in which one serves the church and the larger society. This office serves three ends. First is the procreative end, which is understood by Augustine as raising children for the Kingdom of God. It is not primarily having children of one's own in a biological sense. The second end is the unitive end in which couples learn faithfulness to each other and to God and become thereby witnesses to an 'order of charity.' The third is the sacramental end, which for Augustine relates more often to the indissolubility of marriage.

"These three ends are sustained in the later Middle Ages. While Augustine sees marriage as serving to restrain lust, in the later Middle Ages a more positive view develops in which marriage contributes to growth in holiness...

"The point is that marriage in the Christian tradition serves a number of ends: procreation, fidelity, sacramental, mutual support and companionship, mutual society, and loving companionship. What is striking is that all of these ends can be met by homosexual marriages, even the procreative end when the procreative end is understood as raising children for the Kingdom of God and not primarily as a function of nature [a biological function]. On these grounds, it is appropriate for gay and lesbian Christians to be married in the church, and it is not in violation of Scripture or tradition.

"The objection to this argument by some Christians is to raise up Mark 10:7-8 where Jesus states that 'For this reason a man shall leave his father and mother and be joined to his wife, and the two shall become one flesh.' The argument is then made that this is the only form scriptural marriage can take. The issue addressed in this passage, however, is divorce. Jesus is responding to a hard-hearted test of his authority. Extending his response to a blanket denial of homosexual marriage goes well beyond the text. Moreover, it is uttered by a single Christ who did indeed leave his mother and father to engage in his Incarnate mission. So long as we are dealing with a single Christ who left father and mother for a different reason, we must be open to other possible options, especially options that fulfill the ends of Christian marriage traditionally understood.

"In conclusion, biblical teaching does not address a host of same-sex practices, among them homosexual marriage. Moreover, the ends of marriage as understood in the tradition of the church are ends that homosexual marriage can fulfill. So the issue in the confirmation of a bishop in a homosexual relationship is not whether he or she is gay, not even whether he or she is a practicing homosexual. The question is: is he or she married to this partner, and if so, does this marriage meet these ends."[8]

10

THE SACRAMENT OF SEX

There are those who would say that the topic of homosexuality is really quite simple and just comes down to sex. They might ask, "Isn't the inherent function of sex procreation, an end which homosexual sex does not fulfill?" The 1958 resolution of the Ninth Lambeth Conference (the worldwide gathering of Anglican bishops), on the subject of intercourse affirmed:

> *"Sexual intercourse is not by any means the only language of earthly love, but it is, in its full and right use; the most intimate and the most revealing; it has the depth of communication signified by the Biblical word so often used for it, 'knowledge'; it is a giving and receiving in the unity of two free spirits which is in itself good (within the marriage bond) and mediates good to those who share it. Therefore it is utterly wrong to urge that, unless children are specifically desired, sexual intercourse is of the nature of sin. It is also wrong to say that such intercourse ought not to be engaged in except with the willing intention to procreate children."*[9]

Sex within marriage can fulfill two divine functions: the procreative and the unitive. With regards to these two divine ends of sex (i.e. the procreative and the unitive), if you cannot fulfill one, does that mean you should not do the other? It is like asking, if you are sick and cannot go to church should you not pray? If homosexual sex can fulfill one of the two divine ends of sex, is that not reason enough to bless lifelong homosexual unions/marriages? Interestingly enough, The Roman Catholic Church, as well as most other churches, permits the marriage of infertile couples, as well as the marriage of women past childbearing age, both of which close the possibility of procreation. As Boston College Professor of Theology Charles C. Hefling, Jr. summarizes this beautifully: "Sex can be productive without being reproductive."[10]

11

CONCLUSION

As we have seen, Scripture does not really have much negative to say about the issue of faithful homosexual relationships, or homosexuality for that matter. Furthermore, we have come to see that homosexual sex within a marriage can fulfill one of the divine ends of sex (i.e. the unitive), and that such a marriage also fits within the traditional Christian understanding of the sacrament of marriage—an image of the fidelity and love between God and His Church. I would like to leave you with a short story adapted from an oral rendition by Natalie Graber:

> *Once there was an old man who had to carry water up the hill from the river to his house each day. One of his water jugs, however, had a crack in it, so that, by the time he arrived at the top of the path, most of the water was lost. His neighbors laughed at him: "Why don't you buy a new water jug?" Even his wife criticized him: "Why don't you buy a new water jug?" But the man said nothing.*
>
> *One day, he said to them, "Come with me," and led them, skeptical but curious, down the path that ran from his back door to the river.*
>
> *"Almost every day," said the man to his wide-eyed companions, "on my way to the river, I scatter seeds. On my way home, water leaks from my precious jug to nourish them."*
>
> *To their amazement, the entire left side of path was in bloom. A riot of color—flowers of every hue and tone— made the path a paradise.*

Could it be that homosexuality is similar to that second jug? It may appear broken from a limited and restricted perspective, but truly what appears to be "brokenness" is indeed a hidden virtue. Could one even imagine that the jug is not necessarily "broken," but rather that God, out of abundance and creativity, created more than one type of jug for more than one purpose?

On another note, we accept that it is true that we are not only spiritual and mental beings, but also physical and sexual beings. Does it make sense then that a large percent of God's children should live in denial of a fundamental part of who they are? Should this group be forced to live without the affection and intimacy that comes with committed partnership? Nonetheless, that is precisely what is happening. Homosexuals in the Church are not only among the most marginalized groups, but are often victims of violence or driven to suicide because they cannot make sense of their sexual feelings in the light of what they believe or are told their Bible says. Or because of a lack of understanding of what the Bible truly says (or doesn't say) they are, more often than not, driven to leave the church.

The Church needs to embrace and support homosexuals, not despite scripture and tradition, but in light of it. The doors of the Church need to be opened and human prejudices set aside, so that we can truly live according to the law that Christ taught us. The problem, however, is rooted in fear and lack of awareness. Gomes concludes, "The combination of ignorance and prejudice under the guise of morality makes the religious community, and its abuse of scripture in this regard, itself morally culpable."[11]

For homosexual and heterosexual Christians alike it is imperative to know what the Bible says about homosexuality, as both groups desire to live according to the direction of the Bible, as understood through the life, death, and resurrection of Jesus Christ. With looming constitutional amendments in opposition to homosexual marriage, and division in the larger Church surrounding this issue, it is our responsibility to be as informed as possible. It is my prayer that we may set aside our fears and prejudices and open our minds and hearts to the truth which the Holy Spirit longs to make known to us all. I offer this study as one seeking that truth. May the Spirit of Peace, which surpasses all understanding, guide our hearts and minds as we continue to prayerfully consider this issue.

SOURCES CITED

[1] Siker, Jeffrey, "How to Decide? Homosexual Christians, the Bible and Gentile Inclusions." *Theology Today* 51 (1995), p.221.

[2] *The New American Bible* (World Bible Publishers, Inc., 1987), p.1236.

[3] Blair, Dr. Ralph. Available Online at http://www.ecinc.org/Scriptures/clbrpg.htm

[4] Scroggs, Robin. *The New Testament and Homosexuality: Contextual Background for Contemporary Debate.* (Augsburg Fortress Publishers, 1983), p.120.

[5] Gomes, Peter J. *The Good Book.* (William Morrow & Company, 1996), p.157.

[6] *Ibid.*, p.49-50.

[7] Waskow, Arthur. *Homosexuality and Torah Thought.*

[8] Sample, Tex. *Homosexual Marriage.* Available Online at http://rmnetwork.org/marriage/resources/sample.pdf

[9] *The Family Today: The Report of Committee Five of the Lambeth Conference 1958 Together with the Text of Relevant Resolutions Passed by the Conference* (New York: National Council, Episcopal Church, 1958), p.13.

[10] Gomes, p171.

[11] *Ibid.,* p.147.

RESOURCES

BOOKS

- *What the Bible Really Says About Homosexuality*
  By Daniel A. Helminiak, Ph.D.
  (ISBN: 1-886360-09-X)

- *The Children Are Free: Reexamining the Biblical Evidence on Same-sex Relationships*
  By Rev. Jeff Miner and John Tyler Connoley
  (ISBN: 0-9729396-0-2)

- *Homosexuality and Christian Faith: Questions of Conscience for the Churches*
  Edited by Walter Wink (ISBN: 0-8006-3186-2)

- *Christianity, Social Tolerance, and Homosexuality: Gay People in Western Europe from the Beginning of the Christian Era to the Fourteenth Century*
  By John Boswell (ISBN: 0-22606-711-4)

- *Gay Christian 101: Spiritual Self-Defense For Gay Christians*
  By Rick Brentlinger (ISBN: 978-0-9792461-0-4)

- *Same-Sex Unions in Premodern Europe*
  By John Boswell (ISBN: 0-679-75164-5)

- *Homosexuality in the Orthodox Church*
  By Justin R. Cannon (ISBN: 978-1456416874)

- *Sanctified: An Anthology of Poetry by LGBT Christians*
  Edited by Justin R. Cannon (ISBN: 978-1438247854)

- *Torn: Rescuing the Gospel from the Gays-vs.-Christians Debate*
  By Justin Lee (ISBN: 978-1455514311)

WEBSITES

- **Incusive Orthodoxy** (www.inclusiveorthodoxy.org) - Rev. Cannon's online ministry.

- **Cross2Freedom** (www.cross.2freedom.com) - Rev. Cannon's online bookstore with dozens of books on homosexuality and Christianity.

- **The Gay Christian Network** (www.gaychristian.net) - Support and community for LGBT *Christians* and their friends and family members, plus conferences, podcasts, chats, videos, Bible study, and more.

- **ChristianGays.com** (www.christiangays.com) - A great gay Christian site with products, resources, free personals, chat rooms, and more.

- **GayChurch.org** (www.gaychurch.org) - A really cool site to help you find a gay-friendly church in your area, plus much more.

- **Welcoming Churches** (www.welcomingchurches.com) - A new resource for churches, church staff, and Christians around the country who believe that the Body of Christ should be known for welcoming everyone just as Christ did.

- **Whosoever.org** (www.whosoever.org) - An Online Magazine for LGBT Christians.

APPENDIX

Translations of *malakoi* and *arsenokoitai* in 1 Corinthians 6:9

Bible Version	Year	Translation	
Koine Greek	56	*malakoi*	*arsenokoitai*
Latin Vulgate	405	*molles*	*masculorum concubitores*
Wyclif	1508	lecchouris	synne of Sodom
Tyndale	1525	weaklings	abusers of themselves with mankynde
Great Bible	1539	weaklynges	abusers of themselves with mankynde
Geneva	1560	wantons	bouggerers
Bishops	1568	effeminate	liers with mankinde
Reims-Douai	1609	effeminate	liers with mankind
King James Authorized Version	1611	effeminate	abusers of themselves with mankind
The Revised Version	1811	effeminate	abusers of themselves with men
Darby	1890	those who make women of themselves	abuse themselves with men
Young	1898	effeminate	sodomites
American Standard Version	1901	effeminate	abusers of themselves with men
RVA	1909	los afeminados	los que se echan con varones
Louis Segond	1910	les effimines	les infames
Wesley's NT	1938	guilty of unnatural crime	
Goodspeed	1951	sensual	given to unnatural vice
Jerusalem (French)	1955	effeminate	people with infamous habits
Phillips	1958	effeminate	pervert
Interlinear Greek-	1958	voluptuous	Sodomites

English New Testament		persons	
The Amplified Version	1958	those who participate in homosexuality	
New English	1961	homosexual perversion	
New American Standard	1963	effeminate	homosexuals
Today's English Version	1966	homosexual perverts	
Jerusalem (German)	1968	sissies	child molesters
Jerusalem (English)	1968	Catamites	Sodomites
New American Catholic	1970	homosexual perverts	sodomites
Revised Standard Version	1971	sexual perverts	
The Living Bible	1971	homosexuals	
New International	1973	male prostitutes	homosexual offenders
New King James	1979	homosexuals	sodomites
Rev Luther Bibel	1984	lustknaben	knabenschander
Elberfelder Bibel	1985	Wollustlinge	Knabenschander
New Jerusalem	1985	self indulgent	sodomites
New American Catholic	1987	boy prostitutes	practicing homosexuals
Revised English	1989	sexual pervert	
New Revised Standard	1989	male prostitutes	sodomites
New Living	1996	male prostitutes	homosexuals
Third Millenium	1998	effeminate	abusers of themselves with mankind

Source: http://www.jeramyt.org/gay/gaytrans.html

ABOUT THE AUTHOR

THE REV. JUSTIN R. CANNON is the founding director of Inclusive Orthodoxy (www.InclusiveOrthodoxy.org), a Christian ministry seeking a revitalization of the church that is inclusive of all people in the life and ministry of the church regardless of race, ethnicity, sex, gender, gender identity, or sexual orientation, and also grounded in the scriptures and traditions of the Christian faith.

Rev. Cannon received his Bachelor of Arts from Earlham College and his Master of Divinity from Church Divinity School of the Pacific in Berkeley, CA. He was ordained in The Episcopal Church as a deacon on June 4, 2011 and a priest on December 3, 2011.

Rev. Cannon's work has been featured in *The Advocate*, *New York Times*, and *Los Angeles Times*. In 2006, Rev. Cannon was recognized as one of *OUT Magazine's* Top 100 most influential gay people of the year and in 2007 as one of *Instinct Magazine's* Men of the Year.

He is also the founder and director of a ministry in California called Holy Hikes (www.holyhikes.org) and has a strong interest in eco-theology and environmentalism.

Made in the USA
Lexington, KY
27 June 2013